written by
JEANNE WALKER HARVEY
illustrated by
DIANA TOLEDANO
DRESSING UP THE STARS
The Story of Movie Costume Designer Edith Head
BEACH LANE BOOKS
New York ★ London
Toronto ★ Sydney ★ New Delhi
"Sabrina"
SAMPLE
A
the Sting
Paul
Newman
to each
his own
catch a
thief

Edith was a shy, lonely girl who didn't feel she belonged where she lived. She wanted to be in a place full of people and sounds and dazzling sights.

Instead, she lived near a dusty mine where her stepfather worked. All Edith could see in the distance was a land of stony sand. All she could hear was the whistle of the wind.

To feel less lonely, Edith often hosted make-believe parties for pretend guests, and gave tea parties for her animal friends.

She dressed her black cat, Tom, and her white dog, Dina, in doll clothes. She tied feathers and paper necklaces on her pet jackrabbit and a sleepy horned toad. Edith put ribbons around the middle of burros named Mr. and Mrs. So and So.

Her mother worried when Edith played alone in the desert,
a place with rattlesnakes, scorpions, and tarantulas.

But Edith was brave.

She told her mother,
If I don't bother them, they won't bother me.

Edith's greatest treasure was her bag of fabric scraps. When her family visited the nearest town—called Searchlight, Nevada, four miles away on rugged dirt roads—Edith walked door to door asking for odds and ends.

GENERAL STORE
SALOON

With the scraps, she decorated her dollhouse. She made sofas for pet horned toads. She created hats for the desert cactus.

And best of all, she dressed up her only friends, two sisters who lived in Searchlight. Edith didn't want to appear in her friends' plays. She was bold around rattlesnakes, but not around people. She didn't like her straight hair. Or that she wore glasses.

But she realized the magic power of costumes
when she transformed the girls into their characters.

Edith wished she could transform her life. Every night, she stared at the vast sky of sparkling stars. She dreamed of moving far away from the desert.

Her wish came true when her mother enrolled Edith in a high school in a big, bustling city called Los Angeles.

Excited to be part of this new world, Edith decided she would figure out what she would be when she grew up.

Maybe a concert pianist?

No, the teacher said she had no musical talent.

Maybe a gymnast?

No, Edith tired of repeating the exercises.

But Edith was determined.

She turned her focus to a new passion—*movies*. She escaped feeling shy at school by visiting a big Hollywood movie theater as often as she could.

She lost herself in the stories
of other people's lives.

Edith attended college and became a teacher. But after a few years, the allure of movies drew her back. She landed a job as a sketch artist in a costume department of a Hollywood movie studio, even though she barely knew how to draw.

Luckily, when her boss found out, he didn't fire her. Instead, he laughed and began teaching her how to sketch costumes.

But learning anything new takes time. Early on, Edith was told that her drawing of a dress adorned with feathers "looked like tired spaghetti." A famous actress who saw the sketch said, "Never draw anything like that for me!"

Edith perched by her easel and practiced. Over and over again. Slowly, she improved.

Eventually Edith was directed to make costumes—but not for actors.

Instead, she dressed up animals.
They were not easy clients.

Camels spit at her. Elephants yanked off their decorations. Edith missed her desert toads and burros, who let her adorn them without a fuss.

But Edith was confident.

She told herself she could handle these movie creatures.

And she did just that.

Soon after, Edith got her first big assignment—to create costumes for dancers dressed up as candy at a fancy ball. But her experience was anything but sweet.

The peppermint stick fingernails cracked.
The candy cane stripes dried crooked.
When the dancers sweated, the lollipops stuck together and the chocolate drops melted.

The movie director was furious. Again, Edith almost lost her job.

But Edith convinced the director to give her another chance.

Finally, after many years of hard work, the studio asked Edith to design costumes for famous movie stars. Edith dressed women as sailors, sassy farm girls, and princesses. She dressed men as cowboys, clever crooks, and kings. Just to name a few.

Whenever actresses and actors tried on costumes, Edith wore gray or white or black. She wanted to fade into the background so the movie stars could imagine themselves in their roles.

Sometimes the movie stars or directors argued with her about her costume choices.

But Edith was resolute.

She stood by her designs. After working on hundreds of movies, Edith knew the best ways to develop characters through their costumes. She was famous now, an expert.

Then one star-filled night, Edith arrived at an important ceremony. People recognized her by her distinctive look—her straight, black hair and dark, round glasses. They waved to her beneath the Hollywood searchlights.

When the winner of the Academy Award for Best Costume Design in a movie was announced, Edith was thrilled to hear her name. She climbed the stairs to the stage to accept her award.

And there, standing before movie stars, friends, and admirers, wearing a glamorous gown she had designed for herself . . .

Edith was dazzling.

AUTHOR'S NOTE

As a child growing up in Southern California, I first became fascinated with Edith Head when I watched the Academy Awards filmed in nearby Hollywood. The Academy Awards, also known as the Oscars, are the most prestigious awards in the film industry. My mother and I would always look for the famous costume designer, who was easily recognized by her round dark glasses, blunt haircut, and stylish gowns that she designed for herself.

Although Edith rose to fame in the glamorous world of Hollywood movies, she didn't grow up surrounded by style and fashion. She was born on October 28, 1897, in San Bernardino, California. Her stepfather was a mining engineer, and Edith grew up in remote towns and mining camps in Nevada and Mexico. As an only child, often homeschooled and without playmates nearby, she used her imagination to transform her world.

Eventually, Edith and her mother moved to Los Angeles so she could attend the large public high school there. Edith relished going to the movies at the nearby Million Dollar Theater, the first grand cinema to open in Los Angeles.

Edith went on to study French at the University of California in Berkeley and earn a master's degree in Romance languages from Stanford. She then returned to Southern California to begin her career as a French teacher, first at the Bishop's School in La Jolla, and then at the Hollywood School for Girls in Los Angeles. When asked to also teach art (which she had never studied), Edith attended art classes at night and then shared what she learned with her students the next day. A famous director, Cecil B. DeMille, enrolled his daughters in the Hollywood School for Girls and often invited the students and teachers, including Edith, to the movie studio to watch filming.

Ever drawn to the world of movies, Edith managed to get a costume-

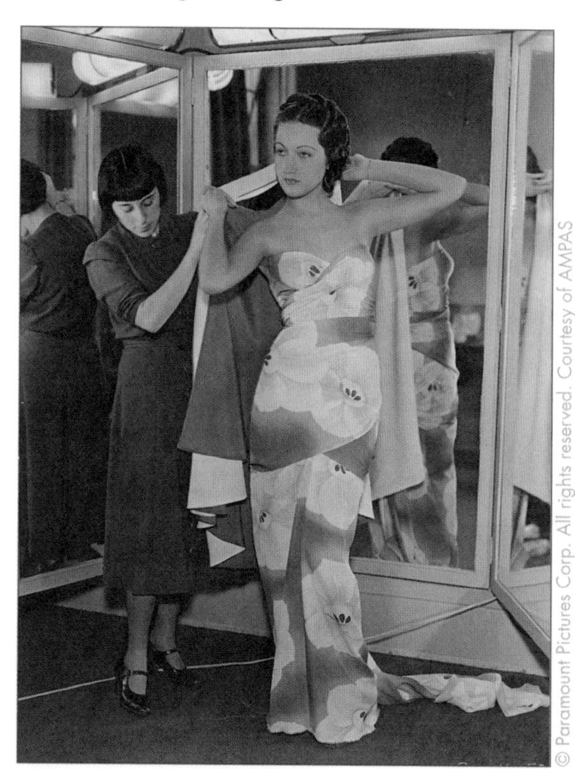

Edith dressing actress Dorothy Lamour, 1938

sketching job with Paramount Studios in 1924, persisting despite her lack of experience. After various early mishaps with her designs, Edith once said that she seriously considered going back to teaching. But she chose to stick it out because, as she wrote, "I was beginning to discover what to me is magic. . . .What a costume designer does is a cross between magic and camouflage. We create the illusion of changing the actors into what they are not."

With her independent spirit, determination, and talent, Edith rose to the top of the male-dominated Hollywood movie costume world as the first female Chief Designer at Paramount Studios.

After working for Paramount Studios for forty-three years, Edith moved to Universal Pictures in 1967 as Chief Designer. At both studios, she gained tremendous respect from famous actors and directors. One actress, Bette Davis, said that Edith was "the queen of her profession. She will never be replaced."

Edith won eight Oscars, more than any other female Oscar winner in history. She was nominated for thirty-five Academy Awards for Best Costume Design, and she designed costumes for hundreds of movies.

"To be a good designer in Hollywood," Edith once said, "one has to be a combination of psychiatrist, artist, fashion designer, dressmaker, pin cushion, historian, nursemaid, and purchasing agent too." Edith was all that, and much more. She was an innovative designer who helped transport viewers into the stories shown onscreen. I think Edith Head, costume designer for the stars, was a star in her own right.

Costume design for Grace Kelly's character in *To Catch a Thief*

Edith at her drafting table at Paramount Pictures

Hollywood agreed. In 1974, Edith received a star on the Hollywood Walk of Fame, where it can be visited today.

In loving memory of my sister, Amy Filice, who delighted in art, design, and style—J. W. H.

Para Elisa, con todo mi amor.
Thanks to Steve and to Isabella, Liza, and Kerri—I couldn't have done it without you—D. T.

Selected Sources

Books

Chierichetti, David. *Edith Head: The Life and Times of Hollywood's Celebrated Costume Designer*. New York: Harper, 2003.

Head, Edith, and Paddy Calistro. *Edith Head's Hollywood*: 25th Anniversary Edition. California: Angel City Press, 2008.

Head, Edith, and Jane Kesner Ardmore. *The Dress Doctor*. New York: Little, Brown, 1959.

Jorgensen, Jay. *Edith Head: The Fifty-Year Career of Hollywood's Greatest Costume Designer*. Pennsylvania: Running Press, 2010.

Websites

"Edith Head Collection Highlights," Academy of Motion Picture Arts and Sciences, https://www.oscars.org/collection-highlights/edith-head. (Featuring highlights from the Margaret Herrick Library and the Academy Film Archive).

"Edith Head," Wisconsin Center for Film and Theater Research, https://www.wisconsinhistory.org/Records?terms=edith+head. (Featuring costume sketches and photos).

BEACH LANE BOOKS An imprint of Simon & Schuster Children's Publishing Division • 1230 Avenue of the Americas, New York, New York 10020 • • For information about special discounts for bulk purchases, please contact Simon & Schuster Special Sales at 1-866-506-1949 or business@simonandschuster.com. • The Simon & Schuster Speakers Bureau can bring authors to your live event. For more information or to book an event, contact the Simon & Schuster Speakers Bureau at 1-866-248-3049 or visit our website at www.simonspeakers.com. • The text for this book was set in Futura. • The illustrations for this book were rendered by hand using many techniques: gouache, collage, colored pencils, crayons, pastels, and more. Edited digitally. • Manufactured in China • 0522 SCP • First Edition • 10 9 8 7 6 5 4 3 2 1 • Library of Congress Cataloging-in-Publication Data • Names: Harvey, Jeanne Walker, author. | Toledano, Diana, illustrator. • Title: Dressing up the stars : the story of movie costume designer Edith Head / Jeanne Walker Harvey ; illustrated by Diana Toledano. • Description: First edition. | New York : Beach Lane Books, [2022] | Audience: Ages: 4-8 | Audience: Grades: 2-3 | Summary: "The story of how Edith Head, who started out as a shy, miner's daughter, became one of the most legendary costume designers in Hollywood"— Provided by publisher. • Identifiers: LCCN 2021018943 (print) | LCCN 2021018944 (ebook) | ISBN 9781534451056 (hardcover) | ISBN 9781534451063 (ebook) • Subjects: LCSH: Head, Edith—Juvenile literature. | Women costume designers—United States—Biography—Juvenile literature. | Costume design—United States—History—Juvenile literature. | Clothing and dress in motion pictures—Juvenile literature. • Classification: LCC TT505.H4 H37 2022 (print) | LCC TT505.H4 (ebook) | DDC 746.9/2092 [B]—dc23/eng/20211006 • LC record available at https://lccn.loc.gov/2021018943 • LC ebook record available at https://lccn.loc.gov/2021018944